YOUR KNOWLEDGE HAS VALUE

AF144806

- We will publish your bachelor's and
  master's thesis, essays and papers

- Your own eBook and book -
  sold worldwide in all relevant shops

- Earn money with each sale

Upload your text at www.GRIN.com
and publish for free

Uqbah Iqbal, Nordin Hussin, Ahmad Ali Seman

The History of the Look-To-The-East Idea in Politics During The Era of Japanese Occupation in Malaya (1941-1945)

The Role of Malai Sinpo Newspaper and Semangat Asia Magazine

GRIN Publishing

Bibliographic information published by the German National Library:

The German National Library lists this publication in the National Bibliography; detailed bibliographic data are available on the Internet at http://dnb.dnb.de .

Imprint:

Copyright © 2014 GRIN Verlag GmbH
Print and binding: Books on Demand GmbH, Norderstedt Germany
ISBN: 978-3-656-86925-2

This book at GRIN:

http://www.grin.com/en/e-book/286506/the-history-of-the-look-to-the-east-idea-in-politics-during-the-era-of

THE HISTORY OF THE LOOK-TO-THE-EAST IDEA IN POLITICS DURING THE ERA OF JAPANESE OCCUPATION IN MALAYA (1941-1945): THE ROLE OF MALAI SINPO NEWSPAPER AND SEMANGAT ASIA MAGAZINE

UQBAH IQBAL[1], NORDIN HUSSIN[2], AHMAD ALI SEMAN[3]

[1]*UQBAH IQBAL
School of History, Politics and Strategy
Faculty of Social Sciences & Humanities,
Universiti Kebangsaan Malaysia, 43650 UKM, Bangi Selangor

[2]NORDIN HUSSIN
School of History, Politics and Strategy
Faculty of Social Sciences & Humanities,
Universiti Kebangsaan Malaysia, 43650 UKM, Bangi Selangor

[3]AHMAD ALI SEMAN
School of History, Politics and Strategy
Faculty of Social Sciences & Humanities,
Universiti Kebangsaan Malaysia, 43650 UKM, Bangi Selangor

*Corresponding Author

ABSTRACT

This study explores the existence of Look-To-The-East idea in Malaya during Japanese occupation era between 1941 and 1945. During this period, the field of journalism and press have been dominated by the Japanese administration or Malayan Military Administration (MMA). Mass communication mediums such as newspapers and magazines have been used as propaganda tools by MMA. Their main purpose was to dominate the field of journalism and press printing to gather people's support in their war campaigns. The government also exploited newspapers and magazines to obtain cooperation from people in all plans they wished to implement. To dominate the field of journalism, MMA had instructed that all efforts related to the publication must obtain prior authorization. Although the printed media

1

in Malaya then was made the propaganda tool by the Japanese administrators, the Look-To-The-East idea was propogated through various newspapers and magazines such as *Berita Malai, Malai Sinpo, Semangat Asia, Suara Timur* and *Fajar Asia*. This study explores the existence of the Look-To-The-East idea that can be found in *Malai Sinpo* newspaper and *Semangat Asia* magazine. It can be divided into politics, social, culture and arts, language, economy, youth, women, family, religion and education areas. This study is centralized upon and focuses on only the politics area.

Keywords: Malai Sinpo, Semangat Asia, Politics, Japan, Look-To-The-East Idea, Malaya

INTRODUCTION

Touching on Japan as a guide to the Malay community during the Japanese occupation era, there were thirty eight studies that cited this issue briefly, among the important one are Muhammad Sa'id bin Haji Sulaiman in his book *Semangat Nippon Yang Sebenarnya Diuraikan*, Muhd. Yusof Ibrahim in an article entitled *Pensejarahan Melayu dalam Zaman Pendudukan Jepun (1942-1945)*, Ishak Saat in an article entitled *Peranan Politik Akhbar Suara Rakyat 1945-48*, Mahani Musa in an article entitled *Sumbangan Wanita Melayu Dalam Kegiatan Persuratkhabaran dan Majalah di Malaysia, Tahun 1920-an 1960-an*, Noraini binti Muhammad in her thesis *Majalah Semangat Asia* and Shaharom Husain in his book *Memoir Shaharom Husain: Selingkar Kenangan Abadi*. This study will give new insights, by gathering all the primary sources for the social area that are available in *Malai Sinpo* newspaper and *Semangat Asia* magazine that led to the formation of the Look-To-The-East idea. The methodology used is based on the observation method of the resources available in libraries and the National Archives of Malaysia. This leads to the reason why this study is important since there were no previous study has been conducted to unearth the existence of the Look-To-The-East idea in *Malai Sinpo* newspaper and *Semangat Asia* magazine. Thus, this is the first study of its kind.

Semangat Asia was first published on 18 January 1943 by Malai Shinbun Sha (Malay Journalism Office), 146 Cecil Street, Singapore. *Semangat Asia* contain Roman alphabet and this newspaper contains page number that is not fixed to each of its publication. It is not more than 34 pages and not less than 28 pages including the advertisements. The price is 15 cents for numbers 1 to 6 and has increased to 25 cents for numbers 8 to 12. Its subscription price for a year is two ringgit. This magazine is a monthly pictorial Roman alphabet Malay language magazine. Among the authors are Ishak Haji Muhammad (Pak Sako), Abdullah Kamel and Abdul Samad Ismail.[1] *Semangat Asia* managed to be published by 17 editions from Volume 1 (numbers 1 to 10) in 1943 and Volume 2 (numbers 1 to 4) in 1944. *Semangat Asia* distributed around all bookstores and journalism representatives in Malaya.

The purpose of *Semangat Asia* publication is to introduce Japan to the residents of Malaya and Sumatra because before the Japanese occupation, only a few of them knows Japan. *Semangat Asia* is also intended to instill the spirit of brotherhood and the close relations between the Asian races, expanding the use of the Japanese and Malay languages, the development of Malay culture and arts and provide a wider reading to all the Malays who are in the city and in the countryside through language and method that are easy to understand. Due to Malaya and Sumatra has been consolidated its administration by the Japanese, the relationship between residents of these regions become more close and strong than ever.[2] *Semangat Asia* expected to paved road leading to this purpose. The publisher and the author of *Semangat Asia* also hoped that the press, members of the literary and intellectual people in Sumatra and Malaya will offer help in meeting the goals of its publication.[3]

Malai Sinpo printed and published by Syonan Sinbun-Kai in 25, Pudu Road, Kuala Lumpur from 1 January 1943 to 31 August 1945. Its editor is Francis Cooray, a Ceylonese journalist in Kuala Lumpur. At this time also, the Axis powers in the Second World War, namely Germany, Italy and Japan were at the peak. *Malai Sinpo* is a daily newspaper published daily except Sunday. The total of its page is between 1 to 3 pages, English language and were priced at 10 cents. Most of its articles are related to the Second World War progress, putting the spirit of fraternity and the close relations between the Asian races, explained the policies of the Japanese authorities in Malaya and expanding the usage of Japanese language.

---

[1] Noraini binti Muhammad, *Majalah Semangat Asia*, Bachelor's Thesis in History, History Department, Faculty of Social Sciences & Humanities, Universiti Kebangsaan Malaysia, 1998, p. 16.

[2] Anon, Telahan Berkenaan Dengan Bahasa Melayu Yang Akan Datang in *Semangat Asia* Number 8, Hachigatsu 2603, p. 1.

[3] Pengarang, Kata Pembuka in *Semangat Asia* Number 1, 18 Ichigatsu 2603, p. 1.

Malai Sinpo is also a propaganda newspaper to get sympathy to Japanese culture and religion and its army who was already conquered Manchuria and almost the entire of Southeast Asia. *Malai Sinpo* also published for the Malays reading in Sumatra since Malaya and Sumatra have been consolidated its administration by Japan. In the author first article on 1 January 2603, *Malai Sinpo* rejected the interpretation of press freedom as understood previously. According to them, the slogan of press freedom does not have meaning at that time if the word freedom means unrestricted license to say anything. In the New Orders that created by Japan, public opinion does not exist separately from the opinion of the country. Newspaper can not exist as a separate country.[4]

Lessons learned from the Look-To-The-East idea in Politics Area

Tengkoe Osman Hussin in article 'Malaisia Dibawah Pimpinan Nippon'[5] and Md. Salehuddin in article 'Kebesaran Kita Dahulu Kala'[6] specify the Malay states history from the past is not so bright and clear for the Malays and historians. Many secrets and books that contain news about the greatness of the Malays from the time of Majapahit and Sriwijaya has been damaged or stored by the West,[7] so that Malay residents don't know the greatness of their ancestor and their cultural height before the Portuguese conquered Malacca. These secrets will be uncovered by Japan so the Malays and Japanese can learn it for their requirement. The Malays urged to learn Japanese language, Japanese history and the spirit of courage sacrifices and loyalty of the Japanese so that they can imitate the progress achieved from these good results. The Malays also prompted to learn the spirit of Japanese Bushido which has made them a race that respected by the world. The Malays have to learn from the Japanese as they seen as an efficient teacher and education received from them will bring good results for the development of the Malays world itself.

---

[4] Mohd. Safar Hasim, *Akhbar dan Kuasa: Perkembangan Sistem Akhbar di Malaysia Sejak 1806*, Kuala Lumpur, Penerbit Universiti Malaya, 1996, p. 205.

[5] Tengkoe Osman Hussin, Malaisia Dibawah Pimpinan Nippon in *Semangat Asia* Number 1, 18 Ichigatsu 2603, p. 15.

[6] Md. Salehuddin, Kebesaran Kita Dahulu Kala in *Semangat Asia* Special Edition of First Anniversary, Number 1 Volume 2, Ichigatsu 2604, pp. 10-12.

[7] See Dr. Rais Yatim, Khazanah Melayu di Belanda in *Mingguan Malaysia*, 13 April 2014, p. 10. Manuscripts and materials of Malay-Indonesia world civilization so much stored at the University of Leiden, at the Royal Tropical Institute, Museum Volkunde, Tropenmuseum and various Dutch, British and German school of humanities.

Inche' Moh. Jihin bin Chor in article 'Riwayat Peprangan Malai'[8] see the history of conflict between Japan and the Western powers by the time of the Second World War and Japanese entry to the Greater East Asia. Japan is said to wage the Greater East Asia War with the goal to establish the Greater East Asia Co-Prosperity Sphere in building a new East Asia area. This article highlights the history narrated by the Japanese victory in the Greater East Asia War. The purpose of the Greater East Asia War also touched by *Semangat Asia* in article 'Tujuan Peperangan Asia Timor Raya'.[9] Pengarang in article 'Susunan Baru: Berdasarkan "Hakko Ichiu" and article "Kema'moran Bersama" Bangsa2 Asia'[10] as well as *Semangat Asia* in article 'Kepada Pemimpin2'[11] as well as *Malai Sinpo* in article 'World Peace in Hand of East Asia'[12] and article 'Spirit of Unity of Asian Races'[13] says Western powers only boasted their civilization through revenue extortion from Asian races. Seen this as a bad things, Japan wage the Greater East Asia War. After the expulsion of Western powers from the region, Asian races urged to get up and work together with strong hearts in setting up Asia.

The duty of the Malay sto develop the Greater East Asia Co-Prosperity Sphere with other Asian races also touched by Thaharuddin A. in article 'Ibu dan Tanah Air'[14] as well as *Malai Sinpo* in article 'Greatest Need of The Moment: To Strengthen Unity of East Asians'[15] and article 'All Races in Malai Are Required To Co-operate: Gunseikan's Message To Malaian

---

[8] Inche' Moh. Jihin bin Chor, Riwayat Peprangan Malai in *Semangat Asia* Special Number, 15 Nigatsu 2603, pp. 17-27.

[9] Anonymous, Tujuan Peperangan Asia Timor Raya in *Semangat Asia* Special Edition of First Anniversary, Number 1 Volume II, Ichigatsu 2604, p. 6.

[10] Pengarang, Susunan Baru: Berdasarkan "Hakko Ichiu" dan "Kema'moran Bersama" Bangsa2 Asia' in *Semangat Asia* Number 4, Shigatsu 2603, pp. 2-4.

[11] Anonymous, Kepada Pemimpin2 in *Semangat Asia* Number 3, Sangatsu 2603, pp. 2-4.

[12] Anonymous, World Peace in Hand of East Asia in *Malai Sinpo* Vol. 4, No. 257, 29 October 2603, p. 1.

[13] Anonymous, Spirit of Unity of Asian Races in *Malai Sinpo* Vol. 4, No. 263, 5 November 2603, p. 1.

[14] Thaharuddin A., Ibu dan Tanah Air in *Semangat Asia* Number 4, Shigatsu 2603, pp. 17-18.

[15] Anonymous, Greatest Need of The Moment: To Strengthen Unity of East Asians in *Malai Sinpo* Vol. 3, No. 164, 12 July 2603, p. 2.

Press Conference'.[16] While Arturo M. Tolentino in article 'Pembenaan Lengkongan Kema'moran Bersama',[17] *Semangat Asia* in article 'Erti Dasar Perbinaan Asia Timor Raya'[18] and article 'Bahagian Kita Bagi Menchapai Kemenangan Akhir',[19] as well as *Malai Sinpo* in article 'Nippon Achieving Aims of Dai Toa Senso: Momentous Changes Intensify Unwavering Solidarity of One Billion of East Asia',[20] article 'Foreign Minister Shigemitsu's Stirring Speech: Six Point Programme for Emancipated Asians in Co-Prosperity Sphere Endorsed'[21] and article 'Ideals of Greater East Asia: Aim At Enduring World Peace'[22] touched on the history of the creation and the purpose of the implementation of the Greater East Asia Co-Prosperity Sphere.

Semangat Asia in article 'Sejarah Asia'[23] take Tenshin Okakura statement in his book entitled 'Chita2 Timor' that stating Asia is one. *Malai Sinpo* in article 'Need for Manifestation of Real Asian Spirit: Unshakable Confidence in Ultimate Victory of Dai Nippon'[24] said this is in line with the Japanese Government's belief that Asian is one and must unite. Japan has taken significant steps to develope all Asian countries and races by giving encouragement and leadership to them. The Japanese victory in the Russo-Japanese War 1904-1905 resulted in a movement to establish a new China, India's independence movement, Indonesian independence, Iran's change movement and others.

---

[16] Anonymous, All Races in Malai Are Required To Co-operate: Gunseikan's Message To Malaian Press Conference in *Malai Sinpo* Vol. 4, No. 240, 9 October 2603, p. 1.

[17] Arturo M. Tolentino, Pembenaan Lengkongan Kema'moran Bersama in *Semangat Asia* Number 8, Hachigatsu 2603, pp. 16-18.

[18] Anonymous, Erti Dasar Perbinaan Asia Timor Raya in *Semangat Asia* Number 10-12, Jugatsu-Junigatsu 2603, p. 1.

[19] Anonymous, Bahagian Kita Bagi Menchapai Kemenangan Akhir in *Semangat Asia* Number 4 Volume II, Shigatsu 2604, pp. 17-18.

[20] Anonymous, Nippon Achieving Aims of Dai Toa Senso: Momentous Changes Intensify Unwavering Solidarity of One Billion People of East Asia in *Malai Sinpo* Vol. 3, No. 182, 3 August 2603, p. 1.

[21] Anonymous, Foreign Minister Shigemitsu's Stirring Speech: Six Point Programme for Emancipated Asians in Co-Prosperity Sphere Endorsed in *Malai Sinpo* Vol. 4, No. 257, 29 October 2603, p. 1.

[22] Anonymous, Ideals of Greater East Asia: Aim At Enduring World Peace in *Malai Sinpo* Vol. 5, No. 339, 3 February 2604, p. 2.

[23] Anonymous, Sejarah Asia in *Semangat Asia* Number 3, Sangatsu 2603, p. 9.

[24] Anonymous, Need for Manifestation of Real Asian Spirit: Unshakable Confidence in Ultimate Victory of Dai Nippon in *Malai Sinpo* Vol. 5, No. 311, 1 January 2604, p. 1.

The rise of nationalism movement in Asia as a result of Japan victory also touched by A. Kamel in article 'Angkatan Muda, Bersi....ap!'[25] as well as *Semangat Asia* in article 'Jika Asia Mahu Bangkit...: Gema perjuangan di-Laut Nippon telah membangkitkan 1,000 milion umat Asia daripada tidor yang nyenyak'[26] and article 'Semangat Yang Memimpin Asia'.[27] The progress of the Russo-Japanese War 1904-1905 also touched by Semangat Asia in article 'Riwayat Perjuangan 27 Gogatsu, 2565',[28] article 'Hari Balatentera'[29] and article 'Lebeh Pelek Daripada Hikayat'.[30] Japanese steps to unify Asia become clearer in the Greater East Asia War. This Asia unification effort touched by *Semangat Asia* in article 'Asia Itu Satu',[31] Ibrahim Haji Ya'acob in article 'Umat Melayu Dari Kurun Kekurun'[32] as well as *Malai Sinpo* in article 'Thai Publicists Entertained in Tokyo: "Asia Is One" Stresses Joho-Kyoku President'[33] and article 'Nippon's Policy Towards East Asia: Will Not Impose Colonial State.'[34]

Semangat Asia in article 'Nippon Memenohi Janjinya Kepada Pendudok2 Rantau Selatan'[35] and article'Chahaya Chemerlang Di-Asia'[36] as well as *Malai Sinpo* in article

---

[25] A. Kamel, Angkatan Muda, Bersi....ap! in *Semangat Asia* Number 5, Gigatsu 2603, p. 2.

[26] Anonymous, Jika Asia Mahu Bangkit...: Gema perjuangan di-Laut Nippon telah membangkitkan 1,000 milion umat Asia daripada tidor yang nyenyak in *Semangat Asia* Number 6, Rokugatsu 2603, pp. 4-7.

[27] Anonymous, Semangat Yang Memimpin Asia in *Semangat Asia* Number 4, Shigatsu 2603, p. 20.

[28] Anonymous, Riwayat Perjuangan 27 Gogatsu, 2565 in *Semangat Asia* Number 6, Rokugatsu 2603, pp. 2-3.

[29] Anonymous, Hari Balatentera in *Semangat Asia* Number 3 Volume II, Sangatsu 2604, pp. 10-11.

[30] Anonymous, Lebeh Pelek Daripada Hikayat in *Semangat Asia* Number 10-12, Jugatsu-Junigatsu 2603, p. 12.

[31] Anonymous, Asia Itu Satu in *Semangat Asia* Number 3, Sangatsu 2603, p. 14.

[32] Ibrahim Haji Ya'acob, Umat Melayu Dari Kurun Kekurun in *Semangat Asia* Number 7, Shichigatsu 2603, pp. 12-13.

[33] Anonymous, Thai Publicists Entertained in Tokyo: "Asia Is One" Stresses Joho-Kyoku President' in *Malai Sinpo* Vol. 3, No. 178, 29 July 2603, p. 1.

[34] Anonymous, Nippon's Policy towards East Asia: Will Not Impose Colonial State in *Malai Sinpo* Vol. 3, No. 201, 25 August 2603, p. 1.

[35] Anonymous, Nippon Memenohi Janjinya Kepada Pendudok2 Rantau Selatan in *Semangat Asia* Number 9, Kugatsu 2603, pp. 12-13.

[36] Anonymous, Chahaya Chemerlang Di-Asia in *Semangat Asia* Special Edition of First Anniversary, Number 1 Volume II, Ichigatsu 2604, p. 5.

'Participation of People in the Administration'[37] and article 'Malaians to Participate in Local Administration: Advisory Council for Each Province and Municipality'[38] state after Malaya's administration become advanced and domestic peace has been restored again, then the Japanese administration decided to establish Consultative Councils and appointing Government officials from the Malays. This was a reply to the cooperation of the Malays in the reconstruction of Malaya. The situation is different with the appointment of Government officials during the British era that only give priority to the rich people, fluently in English and have high position in the society. Japan's policy was to take people who are wise and who aspire to serve the community.

Semangat Asia in article 'Chahaya Chemerlang Di-Asia'[39] state for the first time in the history of the world, has been held a large meeting and full meaning on 5 and 6 Juichigatsu 2603 in Tokyo between independent races in the Greater East Asia. This meeting was attended by the following representatives, the Japanese Government represented by Prime Minister Hideki Tojo, the Chinese Government was represented by President Wang Jingwei (Nanjing Regime), the Thai Government was represented by the Crown Prince Wan Waithayakon, the Manchukuo Government was represented by Prime Minister Zhang Jinghui, the Government of the Philippines was represented by President Jose P. Laurel, the Burmese Government was represented by Prime Minister Dr. Ba Maw and the Indian Government as an observer represented by Subhas Chandra Bose. This meeting is very important means in strengthening the spirit of the whole races in East Asia in the face of war.

The importance of this meeting can be described through 5 decisions reached by consensus among Asian races leaders. The first decision was the Greater East Asia countries will work closely, to ensure the prosperity of their country and establish "The New Order" which has beliefs in common prosperity and security through justice. The second decision was the Greater East Asia countries will determine the direction of their races relations by respecting other Governments and their independence. The third decision is the East Asia

---

[37] Anonymous, Participation of People in the Administration in *Malai Sinpo* Vol. 3, No. 189, 11 August 2603, p.1.

[38] Anonymous, Malaians to Participate in Local Administration: Advisory Council for Each Province and Municipality in *Malai Sinpo* Vol. 4, No. 236, 4 August 2603, p. 2.

[39] Anonymous, Chahaya Chemerlang Di-Asia in *Semangat Asia* Number 10-12, Jugatsu-Junigatsu 2603, pp. 2-4. See also Anonymous, Chahaya Chemerlang Di-Asia in *Semangat Asia* Special Edition of First Anniversary, Number 1 Volume II, Ichigatsu 2604, p. 2.

countries will try to speed up the progress of their economy by collaborating on policy of interest change, and thus will bring prosperity together from their countries. The results of the fourth and the fifth decision is the Greater East Asia countries will develop closer relationship with other countries in the world, and strive to eliminate the differences of race through culture exchange and opening the door of their country to other countries. The next Greater East Asia meeting has been touched by *Malai Sinpo* in article 'Literature of Greater East Asia',[40] article 'Free Asia National Assembly in Tokyo: Momentous Meeting to Plan for the Future'[41] and article 'Magna Charta of East Asia Announced: Joint Declaration by Nations after Tokyo Conference'.[42]

Semangat Asia in article 'Am Persidangan Akhbar Asia Timor Raya',[43] article 'Chahaya Chemerlang Di-Asia'[44] and article 'Malai Baharu'[45] as well as *Malai Sinpo* in article 'Greater East Asia Press Federation Formed: Smashing of Anglo-American Trickery and Intrigues One Object'[46] touched about the Press General Assembly in Tokyo held for three consecutive days, starting from 17 until 19 November 1943. Representatives that involved come from Japan, China, Thailand, Manchukuo, Philippines, Burma, Hong Kong, Borneo, Java, Malaya, Sumatra, Celebes, Serang and French Indochina. On the first day, reporters hearing some speeches from leaders of the Japanese government with respect to their duties in assisting war efforts. On the second day, a resolution was decided to set up a press organisation. On the third day, that organization was formed with the name Greater East Asia Newspaper Alliance.

---

[40] Anonymous, Literature of Greater East Asia in *Malai Sinpo* Vol. 3, No. 206, 30 August 2603, p. 2.

[41] Anonymous, Free Asia National Assembly in Tokyo: Momentous Meeting to Plan for the Future in *Malai Sinpo* Vol. 4, No. 263, 5 November 2603, p. 1.

[42] Anonymous, Magna Charta of East Asia Announced: Joint Declaration by Nations after Tokyo Conference in *Malai Sinpo* Vol. 4, No. 264, 8 November 2603, p. 1.

[43] Anonymous, 'Am Persidangan Akhbar Asia Timor Raya in *Semangat Asia* Number 10-12, Jugatsu-Junigatsu 2603, p. 4.

[44] Anonymous, Chahaya Chemerlang Di-Asia in *Semangat Asia* Special Edition of First Anniversary, Number 1 Volume II, Ichigatsu 2604, pp. 2-3, 5.

[45] Anonymous, Malai Baharu in *Semangat Asia* Number 2, Volume II, Nigatsu 2604, p. 1.

[46] Anonymous, Greater East Asia Press Federation Formed: Smashing of Anglo-American Trickery and Intrigues One Object in *Malai Sinpo* Vol. 4, No. 276, 20 November 2603, p. 1.

Malai Sinpo in article 'To Ensure Definite Victory: Syonan Journalists and Leaders Confer'[47] touched on the conference of reporters and local leaders of Singapore to discuss cooperation with Japan. Later in article 'Empire Celebrates 39th Army Day To-Day',[48] article 'Day of Rejoicing and Prayer: Anniversary of Brilliant Victory of Battle of Mukden',[49] article 'Empire Celebrates 39th Army Day Day To-Day: Army Is The Nippon Nation'[50] and article 'Dai Toa Celebrates Army Day: Colourful Programme in Empire's Capital',[51] *Malai Sinpo* said Japanese troops should always commemorate their victory in the past fighting during the critical moment of war to raise their courage spirit.

Conclusion

Putting Japan as an example and a role model can be viewed as a form of Look-To-The-East idea that has been initiated since the beginning of the 20th century. It was the Kaum Muda who initiated it through the publication of *al-Imam* magazine in July 1906 and subsequently, this idea was expanded by other newspapers and magazines during the British colonial era. After Japan had successfully driven the British out of Malaya, the Look-To-The-East idea was still continued by the Japanese government during the Second World War through the publication of *Malai Sinpo* newspaper and *Semangat Asia* magazine. *Malai Sinpo* and *Semangat Asia* were also published for the reading of the Malays in Indonesia, making use of the standardized Malay language in the paper for the Malays in Malaya and Indonesia.

Although there are various areas can be found in *Malai Sinpo and Semangat Asia*, this paper only deals with politics area. Look-To-The-East idea adopted in the Malay community life at this time comprised of various aspects. For example, the Malays urged to learn

---

[47] Anonymous, To Ensure Definite Victory: Syonan Journalists and Leaders Confer in *Malai Sinpo* Vol. 10, No. 807, 2 June 2605, p. 1.

[48] Anonymous, Empire Celebrates 39th Army Day To-day in *Malai Sinpo* Vol. 5, No. 370, 10 March 2604, p. 1.

[49] Anonymous, Day of Rejoicing and Prayer: Anniversary of Brilliant Victory of Battle of Mukden in *Malai Sinpo* Vol. 5, No. 370, 10 March 2604, p. 1.

[50] Anonymous, Empire Celebrates 39th Army Day To-Day: Army Is The Nippon Nation in *Malai Sinpo* Vol. 5, No. 370, 10 March 2604, p. 2.

[51] Anonymous, Dai Toa Celebrates Army Day: Colourful Programme in Empire's Capital in *Malai Sinpo* Vol. 5, No. 371, 11 March 2604, p. 1.

Japanese language, Japanese history and the spirit of courage sacrifices and loyalty of the Japanese so that they can imitate the progress achieved from this good results, the Malays prompted to wake up and work together with strong hearts in setting up Asia, the independence races meeting in the Greater East Asia, the Press General Assembly in Tokyo and the conference of reporters and local leaders of Singapore to discuss cooperation with Japan.

PRIMARY RESOURCES

A. Kamel. 2603. Angkatan Muda, Bersi....ap!. *Semangat Asia* Number 5, Gigatsu: 2.

Anonymous. 2603. Kepada Pemimpin2. *Semangat Asia* Number 3, Sangatsu: 2-4.

Anonymous. 2603. Sejarah Asia. *Semangat Asia* Number 3, Sangatsu: 9.

Anonymous. 2603. Asia Itu Satu. *Semangat Asia* Number 3, Sangatsu: 14.

Anonymous. 2603. Semangat Yang Memimpin Asia. *Semangat Asia* Number 4, Shigatsu: 20.

Anonymous. 2603. Riwayat Perjuangan 27 Gogatsu, 2565. *Semangat Asia* Number 6, Rokugatsu: 2-3.

Anonymous. 2603. Jika Asia Mahu Bangkit...: Gema perjuangan di-Laut Nippon telah membangkitkan 1,000 milion umat Asia daripada tidor yang nyenyak. *Semangat Asia* Number 6, Rokugatsu: 4-7.

Anonymous. 2603. Telahan Berkenaan Dengan Bahasa Melayu Yang Akan Datang. *Semangat Asia* Number 8, Hachigatsu: 1.

Anonymous. 2603. Nippon Memenohi Janjinya Kepada Pendudok2 Rantau Selatan. *Semangat Asia* Number 9, Kugatsu: 12-13.

Anonymous. 2603. Erti Dasar Perbinaan Asia Timor Raya. *Semangat Asia* Number 10-12, Jugatsu-Junigatsu: 1.

Anonymous. 2603. Chahaya Chemerlang Di-Asia. *Semangat Asia* Number 10-12, Jugatsu-Junigatsu: 2-4.

Anonymous. 2603. 'Am Persidangan Akhbar Asia Timor Raya. *Semangat Asia* Number 10-12, Jugatsu-Junigatsu: 4.

Anonymous. 2603. Lebeh Pelek Daripada Hikayat. *Semangat Asia* Number 10-12, Jugatsu-Junigatsu: 12.

Anonymous. 2603. Greatest Need of The Moment: Tp Strengthen Unity of East Asians. *Malai Sinpo* Vol. 3, No. 164, 12 July: 2.

Anonymous. 2603. Thai Publicists Entertained in Tokyo: "Asia Is One" Stresses Joho-Kyoku President'. *Malai Sinpo* Vol. 3, No. 178, 29 July: 1.

Anonymous. 2603. Nippon Achieving Aims of Dai Toa Senso: Momentous Changes Intensify Unwavering Solidarity of One Billion People of East Asia. *Malai Sinpo* Vol. 3, No. 182, 3 August: 1.

Anonymous. 2603. Participation of People in the Administration. *Malai Sinpo* Vol. 3, No. 189, 11 August: 1.

Anonymous. 2603. Nippon's Policy towards East Asia: Will Not Impose Colonial State. *Malai Sinpo* Vol. 3, No. 201, 25 August: 1.

Anonymous. 2603. Literature of Greater East Asia. *Malai Sinpo* Vol. 3, No. 206, 30 August: 2.

Anonymous. 2603. Greater East Asia Press Federation Formed: Smashing of Anglo-American Trickery and Intrigues One Object. *Malai Sinpo* Vol. 4, No. 276, 20 November: 1.

Anonymous. 2603. Malaians to Participate in Local Administration: Advisory Council for Each Province and Municipality. *Malai Sinpo* Vol. 4, No. 236, 4 August: 2.

Anonymous. 2603. All Races in Malai Are Required To Co-operate: Gunseikan's Message To Malaian Press Conference. *Malai Sinpo* Vol. 4, No. 240, 9 October: 1.

Anonymous. 2603. World Peace in Hand of East Asia. *Malai Sinpo* Vol. 4, No. 257, 29 October: 1.

Anonymous. 2603. Foreign Minister Shigemitsu's Stirring Speech: Six Point Programme for Emancipated Asians in Co-Prosperity Sphere Endorsed. *Malai Sinpo* Vol. 4, No. 257, 29 October: 1.

Anonymous. 2603. Spirit of Unity of Asian Races. *Malai Sinpo* Vol. 4, No. 263, 5 November: 1.

Anonymous. 2603. Free Asia National Assembly in Tokyo: Momentous Meeting to Plan for the Future. *Malai Sinpo* Vol. 4, No. 263, 5 November: 1.

Anonymous. 2603. Magna Charta of East Asia Announced: Joint Declaration by Nations after Tokyo Conference. *Malai Sinpo* Vol. 4, No. 264, 8 November: 1.

Anonymous. 2604. Chahaya Chemerlang Di-Asia. *Semangat Asia* Special Edition of First Anniversary, Number 1 Volume II, Ichigatsu: 2.

Anonymous. 2604. Chahaya Chemerlang Di-Asia. *Semangat Asia* Special Edition of First Anniversary, Number 1 Volume II, Ichigatsu: 5.

Anonymous. 2604. Chahaya Chemerlang Di-Asia. *Semangat Asia* Special Edition of First Anniversary, Number 1 Volume II, Ichigatsu: 2-3, 5.

Anonymous. 2604. Tujuan Peperangan Asia Timor Raya. *Semangat Asia* Special Edition of First Anniversary, Number 1 Volume II, Ichigatsu: 6.

Anonymous. 2604. Malai Baharu. *Semangat Asia* Number 2, Volume II, Nigatsu: 1.

Anonymous. 2604. Hari Balatentera. *Semangat Asia* Number 3 Volume II, Sangatsu: 10-11.

Anonymous. 2604. Bahagian Kita Bagi Menchapai Kemenangan Akhir. *Semangat Asia* Number 4 Volume II, Shigatsu: 17-18.

Anonymous. 2604. Need for Manifestation of Real Asian Spirit: Unshakable Confidence in Ultimate Victory of Dai Nippon. *Malai Sinpo* Vol. 5, No. 311, 1 January: 1.

Anonymous. 2604. Ideals of Greater East Asia: Aim At Enduring World Peace. *Malai Sinpo* Vol. 5, No. 339, 3 February: 2.

Anonymous. 2604. Empire Celebrates 39th Army Day To-day. *Malai Sinpo* Vol. 5, No. 370, 10 March: 1.

Anonymous. 2604. Day of Rejoicing and Prayer: Anniversary of Brilliant Victory of Battle of Mukden. *Malai Sinpo* Vol. 5, No. 370, 10 March: 1.

Anonymous. 2604. Empire Celebrates 39th Army Day To-Day: Army Is The Nippon Nation. *Malai Sinpo* Vol. 5, No. 370, 10 March: 2.

Anonymous. 2604. Dai Toa Celebrates Army Day: Colourful Programme in Empire's Capital. *Malai Sinpo* Vol. 5, No. 371, 11 March: 1.

Anonymous. 2605. To Ensure Definite Victory: Syonan Journalists and Leaders Confer. *Malai Sinpo* Vol. 10, No. 807, 2 June: 1.

Arturo M. Tolentino. 2603. Pembenaan Lengkongan Kema'moran Bersama. *Semangat Asia* Number 8, Hachigatsu: 16-18.

Dr. Rais Yatim. 2014. Khazanah Melayu di Belanda. *Mingguan Malaysia*, 13 April: 10.

Ibrahim Haji Ya'acob. 2603. Umat Melayu Dari Kurun Kekurun. *Semangat Asia* Number 7, Shichigatsu: 12-13.

Inche' Moh. Jihin bin Chor. 2603. Riwayat Peprangan Malai. *Semangat Asia* Special Number, 15 Nigatsu: 17-27.

Md. Salehuddin. 2604. Kebesaran Kita Dahulu Kala. *Semangat Asia* Special Edition of First Anniversary, Number 1 Volume Jilid II, Ichigatsu: 10-12.

Pengarang. 2603. Kata Pembuka. *Semangat Asia* Number 1, 18 Ichigatsu: 1.

Pengarang. 2603. Susunan Baru: Berdasarkan "Hakko Ichiu" dan "Kema'moran Bersama" Bangsa2 Asia'. *Semangat Asia* Number 4, Shigatsu: 2-4.

Tengkoe Osman Hussin. 2603. Malaisia Dibawah Pimpinan Nippon. *Semangat Asia* Number 1, 18 Ichigatsu: 15.

Thaharuddin A. 2603. Ibu dan Tanah Air. *Semangat Asia* Number 4, Shigatsu: 17-18.

SECONDARY SOURCES

Ishak Saat. (2010). Peranan Politik Akhbar Suara Rakyat 1945-48. *Kemanusiaan* 17, 65-89.

Mahani Musa. (2011). Sumbangan Wanita Melayu Dalam Kegiatan Persuratkhabaran dan Majalah di Malaysia, Tahun 1920-an 1960-an (Abdul Rahman Haji Ismail & Mahani Musa (editors), *Akhbar dan Tokoh Persuratkhabaran Malaysia Kurun ke-20*, pp. 64-82). Pulau Pinang: Universiti Sains Malaysia Publisher.

Mohd. Safar Hasim. 1996. *Akhbar dan Kuasa: Perkembangan Sistem Akhbar di Malaysia Sejak 1806.* Kuala Lumpur: Penerbit Universiti Malaya.

Muhammad Said bin Haji Sulaiman (Translation). (1942). *Semangat Nippon Yang Sebenarnya Diuraikan.* No place: Sheikh bin Alwi Shahab.

Muhd. Yusof Ibrahim. (1996). Pensejarahan Melayu dalam Zaman Pendudukan Jepun (1942-1945). *Jebat: Malaysian Journal of History, Politics and Strategic Studies* 24, 109-118.

Noraini binti Muhammad. (1998). *Majalah Semangat Asia*. Bachelor's Degree Thesis in History. History Dept, The Faculty of Social Science and Humanity, Universiti Kebangsaan Malaysia.

Shaharom Husain. (1985). *Biografi Perjuangan Politik Dato' Onn Ja'afar*. Petaling Jaya: Penerbit Fajar Bakti Sdn. Bhd.